3

A Dog for Each Day

Written by Lynea Bowdish
Illustrated by Karen Stormer Brooks

Children's Press
A Division of Scholastic Inc.
New York • Toronto • London • Auckland • Sydney
Mexico City • New Delhi • Hong Kong
Danbury, Connecticut

For Chipper, with love from Lynea, David, and Princess

For Connor and Holly
—K.S.B.

Reading Consultants

Linda Cornwell
Literacy Specialist

Katharine A. Kane
Education Consultant
(Retired, San Diego County Office of Education
and San Diego State University)

Library of Congress Cataloging-in-Publication Data

Bowdish, Lynea.
    A dog for each day / written by Lynea Bowdish ; illustrated by
Karen Stormer Brooks.
        p. cm. — (Rookie reader)
Summary: Describes Bertha McCain's seven dogs, one for each day
of the week.
    ISBN 0-516-22849-8 (lib. bdg.)   0-516-27399-X (pbk.)
    [1. Dogs—Fiction. 2. Pets—Fiction. 3. Stories in rhyme.] I. Brooks,
Karen Stormer, ill. II. Title. III. Series.
    PZ8.3.B6725 Do 2003
    [E]—dc21
                                2002008781

CHILDREN'S PRESS, AND A ROOKIE READER®, and associated logos are trademarks
and or registered trademarks of Grolier Publishing Co., Inc. SCHOLASTIC and
associated logos are trademarks and or registered trademarks of Scholastic Inc.
1 2 3 4 5 6 7 8 9 10 R 12 11 10 09 08 07 06 05 04 03

Seven dogs live
with Bertha McCain.

"Seven's too many," her neighbors complain.

But Bertha McCain
says all seven will stay.

With seven,
she has a dog for each day.

**Monday's dog
always barks at the cat.**

Tuesday's dog
brings Bertha's blue hat.

**Wednesday's dog
likes to go get the mail.**

Thursday's dog
makes a breeze with his tail.

Friday's dog
keeps Bertha's feet warm.

**Saturday's dog
likes to howl a song.**

Sunday's dog
wakes up Bertha at nine.

All seven help get her
to church, and on time!

And if they get lonely,
Bertha is sure,

they'll be able to squeeze in
at least seven more.

Word List (74 words)

a	dogs	live	Sunday's
able	each	lonely	sure
all	feet	mail	tail
always	for	makes	the
and	Friday's	many	they
at	get	McCain	they'll
barks	go	Monday's	Thursday's
be	has	more	time
Bertha	hat	neighbors	to
Bertha's	help	nine	too
blue	her	on	Tuesday's
breeze	his	Saturday's	up
brings	howl	says	wakes
but	if	seven	warm
cat	in	seven's	Wednesday's
church	is	she	will
complain	keeps	song	with
day	least	squeeze	
dog	likes	stay	

About the Author

Lynea Bowdish has been lucky enough to know and love a lot of dogs. She and her husband, David Roberts, live in Hollywood, Maryland, with Princess, who is mostly beagle. They also share their home with a large goldfish and an algae eater.

Lynea would have a dog for every day of the year if she could, but Princess and David think that 365 dogs are too many. They may be right.

About the Illustrator

Karen Stormer Brooks lives and works in Atlanta, Georgia, with her husband, Scott, who is also an illustrator. They have two children, Connor and Holly, who would like to have a dog. They have two cats who would not.